Ryedale Pilgrimage

Ryedale Pilgrimage

by

David Goodall

David Goodall

Maxiprint
2000

ISBN 1 871125 47 2

Published, designed and printed on behalf of
The Leonard Cheshire Foundation
by Maxiprint (York) Limited
Kettlestring Lane
York, England
YO30 4XF

www.maxiprint.co.uk

Contents

Bransdale 120

NORTHALLERTON

100 **Leake**

28 **Hawnby**

East Moors 70

Hutton-le-Hole

18 **Lastingham**

8 **Appleton-le-Moors**

Carlton 96

Old Byland 82

Pockley

Kirkdale 92

Kirkbymoorside

40 **Sinnington**

PICKERING

Cold Kirby 94

Rievaulx 2

54

North Kilvington

Thirsk

50 **Scawton**

Helmsley 36

Harome

Normanby

48 **Salton**

Kirby Misperton

24 **Sproxton**

Bagby 14

Thirkleby 114

Kilburn 10

Ampleforth

86 78 **Oswaldkirk**

Nunnington 42

131 117 **Byland**

Gilling East 6

Stonegrave 64

Slingsby

Coxwold 108

Carlton Husthwaite 38

Hovingham 68

52

Baldersby 72

Husthwaite 20

112 **Appleton-le-Street**

74 **Old Malton**

Topcliffe 60

Rainton

Sessay 32

MALTON

Brandsby 16

Dalby 62

Terrington

RIPON

Raskelf 102

Helperby

Easingwold

Crayke 30

Stillington 124

Marton-in-the-Forest 104

Farlington

Bulmer

Whitwell-on-the-Hill 126

Skelton-on-Ure 128

Boroughbridge

106 **Alne**

Huby

Sheriff Hutton 80

Aldwark

46

Tollerton

Sutton-on-the-Forest 84

Flaxton

26 **Howsham**

58 **Little Ouseburn**

Linton-on-Ouse

Strensall

90 **Skelton**

74 **Old Malton**
Location and page number
of Featured Churches

Dedications of Featured Churches

All Saints/All Hallows	10	St Gregory	1
St Mary	9	St Helen and the Holy Cross	1
Blessed Virgin Mary	2	St Hilda	1
Holy Trinity	2	St James the Great	1
St Cuthbert	2	St John	1
St Michael	2	St John Baptist	1
St Nicholas	2	St John of Beverley	1
All Saints and St James	1	St John the Evangelist	1
Christ Church	1	St Laurence	1
Christ the Consoler	1	St Mary Magdalene	1
Holy Cross	1	St Mary the Virgin	1
St Aidan	1	St Nicholas and St Mary	1
St Chad	1	St Oswald	1
St Columba	1	St Peter	1
St Giles	1	St Stephen	1

Ryedale Pilgrimage
A Tour of North Yorkshire Churches

More than fifty years ago, a group of boys at Ampleforth College, under the inspiration of the late Father Columba Cary-Elwes (then a Housemaster), produced a little guidebook to the neighbourhood called *The Ampleforth Country*. Each of us was allotted two or three villages to research and describe. So in the Summer Term of 1947 a friend and I set off into the Ryedale countryside on bicycles, talking to Vicars and local residents and then amplifying and correcting what we had gleaned by reference to *The Victoria County History*.

In the immediate aftermath of the War, the roads were virtually free of motor traffic; agriculture had not yet become agro-industry; tourism was minimal; gentrification of the villages had not yet begun. So we had the privilege of exploring and experiencing an essentially nineteenth century countryside - a countryside which, as the preface to the first edition of *The Ampleforth Country* proudly claimed, bore "vivid evidence to the sweep of English history in such a variety of landscape as (exists) nowhere else in England."

With the great Benedictine Abbey of Ampleforth at its centre, the Ryedale countryside made an impression on me which never faded during a career spent away from Yorkshire, in London and overseas. When, in 1971, my wife and I felt the need of a base for the family in our peripatetic life, we bought a holiday cottage at Ampleforth; and when the time came to retire in 1991, we had no hesitation about deciding to make it our permanent home. It then became possible to re-explore, this time with the aid of a sketchpad and a box of watercolours, the enchanted landscape which I first came to know as a schoolboy half a century earlier. This book of watercolour drawings is the result.

The seed of an interest in watercolours was planted in me at school, in what was then known as "extra art". But it was not until twenty years later that the seed bore fruit in the shape of a desire to capture something of the flavour of the landscapes and buildings around me.

First attempts were profoundly discouraging; but the desire persisted. I kept trying, and eventually there came a day when some faint correspondence appeared between the view I was drawing and what I had put on paper; and from then on I was hooked. Since then the hobby has accompanied me on my postings round the world from Austria and Germany to India. The results have no pretensions to be other than very amateur work; but producing them has afforded me many hours of pleasure: intervals of detachment and sanity amid the stresses of diplomatic life.

Much has changed in Ryedale and its surrounding areas since the 1940s, not least the ubiquity of the motorcar (and in summer the caravan). Disproportionately titanic buses and heavy goods vehicles thunder along its narrow roads and through its villages. Profiteering developers have surrounded the small market towns with a penumbra of assembly-line housing estates. But this Northern landscape of gentle hills and valleys, of alternating moorland, farmland and forest, retains its profoundly rural character and its fundamental tranquillity. Here solitude – an increasingly rare and expensive commodity in much of our overcrowded island – is still within easy reach of everyone's front door.

The tide of paganism and cynicism which has coarsened our national life is less apparent in the countryside than in the cities, and the rural landscape is still impregnated with thirteen centuries of Christianity. In the seventh century, what is now Yorkshire formed part of the kingdom of Northumbria, where St Paulinus brought the Gospel and converted King Edwin. Just across the River Derwent from Malton occurred the famous episode related by Bede, when the king listened to one of his counsellors comparing the life of man to a sparrow flying through the hall and "vanishing into the wintry world from which he came. Even so, man appears on earth for a little while; but of what went before this life or of what follows, we know nothing. Therefore if this new teaching (Christianity) has brought more certain knowledge, it seems right to follow it."

The Venerable Bede would still recognise the map of Ryedale and many of the places in it, not least Lastingham, where he records the building of a monastery by Cynibil the priest at the request of his brother Cedd, from whom the abbacy passed to a third brother, Chad. St Chad's monastery was destroyed by the Danes, but the eleventh century crypt which stands in its place today can still carry the imagination back far beyond it to the mission of Paulinus, and further back still to earliest days of Christianity in England.

The churches portrayed here are not confined exclusively to Ryedale, or even to North Yorkshire. Little Ouseburn and Skelton-on-Ure (Newby) are across the county boundary in West Yorkshire, while Howsham is in East Yorkshire. The area covered has Ampleforth at its centre and extends roughly from Malton in the east to Newby in the west, and from Bransdale in the north to Skelton, near York, in the south. Even here there are many

omissions, and I apologise to readers whose favourite churches do not appear. I have followed no principle of selection, and simply sketched where chance and fancy led me.

At the suggestion of Suzie Gordon, I have included a church for every week of the year; but here again it has been impossible to order them on any consistent principle. I thought at first that it might be done by reference to the feast day of the saint or saints to whom the church is dedicated. But then I found that no less than eleven were dedicated to All Saints and a further eleven to St Mary or the Blessed Virgin Mary. So the ordering is a compromise: where possible, a church appears close either to its patronal feast day or else to the date on which the drawing was made. In other cases, a church has simply been slotted in to fill a vacant space in the calendar.

Except for the ruined abbey churches of Rievaulx and Byland, and the modern abbey church at Ampleforth, the churches I have chosen are not great churches. There is little here of the scale or splendour of the rich wool churches of East Anglia or the West Country. They are for the most part modest structures, built, added to and restored over the centuries to serve small village communities. The majority originated before the Norman Conquest and contain traces of almost every period of architecture since. As everywhere else in England, the hand of the Victorian restorer is much in evidence; and there are several complete examples of high Victorian work, notably William Burges' sumptuous church of Christ the Consoler at Newby, Butterfield's soaring spire at Baldersby, G.E.Street's Gothic cameo at Howsham and E.B.Lamb's exuberantly eccentric essays at Thirkleby, Aldwark and Bagby.

Individually, perhaps only Lastingham, because of its crypt, and Kirkdale, with its celebrated Anglo-Saxon inscription, are of national significance. But taken together, they provide a conspectus of the English village church and its development from Saxon times to the twentieth century; and each of them has its own features of historical interest and its own distinctive charm.

Remarkably, none of them is in disrepair. A few of them, sadly, have to be kept locked because of vandalism and theft. But however far off the beaten track, however small and scattered the congregation which supports it, virtually every church shown here is cared for and in at least occasional use, a place where (in Betjeman's words) "the Faith is taught and the sacraments administered". Which is why visiting and drawing them has not only given me much enjoyment, but has also had something of the character of a pilgrimage.

It hardly needs to be said that this is in no sense an architectural or historical guide to the churches concerned. There is nothing systematic about it: I have simply drawn attention to aspects of each church or locality which caught my fancy or my interest. Nevertheless, the commentary could not have been written without frequent reference to the volumes on the North, East and West Ridings of Yorkshire in the late Professor Nikolaus Pevsner's *Buildings of England*, and to the *Victoria County History* of the North Riding. To both of these monumental repositories of information I am heavily in debt; and I am grateful to Penguin UK for permission quote from the former. I have also drawn unashamedly on

Mr Thomas Gill's *Vallis Eboracensis* of 1852 and the 4th (Enlarged) edition of *The Ampleforth Country*, which appeared in 1966; and I am grateful to John Murray (Publishers) Ltd for permission to quote from the late John Betjeman's poem *Perp. Revival i' the North*.

My special thanks are due to Fr Edward Corbould of Ampleforth who first suggested the idea of this book; to Professor Patrick Nuttgens, who encouraged and facilitated it; and to Suzie Gordon and Geoffrey Geddes of Maxiprint, who have made it a reality. It is dedicated to my wife Morwenna; to our children Elisabeth, Dominic and John; and along with them to the memory of Leonard Cheshire, whose life of active service to disabled people was sustained by prayer in quiet places.

January

The Abbey of the Blessed Virgin Mary at Rievaulx

There may well have been snow on the ground at the beginning of March in the year 1132, when the founding party of twelve monks from St Bernard's abbey of Clairvaux in France arrived in this desolate valley, set in a countryside still wasted and depopulated by William the Conqueror's "harrowing of the North". It must have been a chilly and discouraging start for what was soon to become one of the greatest and most celebrated of the English Cistercian houses.

What we see today as a tranquil and romantic site amid hills and woodland appeared very differently to twelfth century eyes: according to the contemporary chronicler William of Newburgh, the monks settled "*in loco horroris at vastae solitudinis*": in a place of horror and great loneliness. But the Cistercians' life of silence and prayer - carried on in England today at Mount St Bernard's Abbey in Leicestershire - is also a life of industry; and in the Middle Ages they specialised in taming desolate landscapes and making them productive.

St Bernard's reputation for sanctity and the contemporary climate of monastic and church reform meant that there was no shortage of dedicated Cistercian recruits. Within thirty five years of its foundation, under its third and greatest abbot, St Aelred, the monastic community at Rievaulx numbered 140 choir monks and as many as 500 lay brothers. The foundation at Rievaulx was soon followed by another at Fountains, and then by Byland and Jervaulx, making North Yorkshire famous as a centre of Cistercian life. Fountains became the largest and richest of the four, but Rievaulx at its zenith was not far behind.

For two hundred years after its foundation, Rievaulx flourished. But in 1332 the Abbey was plundered by a marauding Scottish Army - a perennial hazard for medieval

Rievaulx

AS 9. ii. 99

monasteries in the North of England – and the Black Death which decimated the population in the 1340s afflicted all the monasteries and weakened the Church across the whole of Europe. The Abbot of Rievaulx continued to rank as one of the major landowners of the North Riding, and additions continued to be made to the splendid range of buildings whose ruins survive. But monastic fervour gradually declined, along with the number of vocations to the monastic life; and by the 1530s the community was down to 24 monks.

In 1538, along with the other "Greater Monasteries", Rievaulx was dissolved by Henry VIII. The roofs were stripped of their lead, the buildings despoiled and some deliberately destroyed; and the ruins became a quarry from which many of the local cottages were built. Of the great church, as large as a cathedral, the Norman nave has all but disappeared, only the stumps of the pillars and traces of the side-chapels being still visible. What remain standing are the transepts, linked by the noble arch of the crossing, together with the thirteenth century monks' choir and chancel.

The life of prayer has not wholly disappeared from Rievaulx. The gatehouse chapel of the abbey was restored to serve as the village church in 1906 by Temple Moore (1856-1920), who had a hand in so many Ryedale churches; and adjoining it is a small Anglican convent. Services are sometimes held in the ruined choir; and the monks from nearby Ampleforth sing vespers there on special occasions. For its beauty, its history and its associations, and for the aura of contemplative prayer which still clings to its ruins, this seems the right place at which to begin a year's pilgrimage round the churches of North Yorkshire.

Not surprisingly, Rievaulx has always been a favourite with watercolourists. Deep in its wooded valley and well away from any large centre of population, it still looks very much as it did when Cotman and Girtin painted it at the beginning of the 19th century. Conscious of these illustrious predecessors, an amateur approaches it with extreme diffidence. This view was done on the spot, and neither the near-arctic temperature nor my wife (who was sitting patiently in the car) encouraged loitering. But with watercolours it is often the least laboured which come out best, and I felt that this quick sketch managed to catch the mood of the moment.

Holy Cross, Gilling

This distant view of Gilling Church in melting snow is from the Oswaldkirk road, done on a raw winter afternoon. Gilling Castle, now the Ampleforth College Junior School, is just out of sight in the woods to the right.

The church tower is late 16th century, but the body of the church was originally Norman, the chancel being rebuilt in the 14th century. Prince Ranjitsihji, the celebrated cricketer, who was a frequent visitor to Gilling (where the Rector had been his tutor), raised the money for the church clock by means of cricket matches and set the clock going himself.

The history of the church is bound up with the Fairfax family, cousins to the Cholmeleys at Brandsby (see p.16), who lived at Gilling Castle for more than four hundred years; and the church contains several memorials to them

The most notable are the three lifesize effigies of Sir Thomas Fairfax (who died in 1572) and his two wives, and a fine classical figure "of Piety, reclining", in memory of Thomas Fairfax who died in 1828 aged 29, by Joseph Gott, an English sculptor living in Rome.

The Rectory of Gilling was in the gift of the Master and Fellows of Trinity College, Cambridge; and as their memorials in and around the church testify, a whole succession of rectors maintained the tradition of the scholar-parson, having started their careers as Fellows and Tutors at Trinity. The transition from University life to life in the country seems to have done them no harm, several memorials recording incumbencies of more than thirty years.

27·2·93

GILLING

Christ Church, Appleton-le-Moors

An uncompromisingly Victorian essay by J.L.Pearson (1817-97), later the architect of Truro Cathedral. Erected in 1863-5 by a Mrs Shepherd in memory of her husband (a local man who began his life as a cabin-boy and ended it as a wealthy shipowner), no expense was spared in its construction, which cost the then very considerable sum of £10,000. The result is a dignified exterior and an interior into which has been packed virtually every decorative or sculptured feature which a Gothic Revival architect could think of. The contrast with the stern simplicity of Lastingham (p.18), which Pearson restored and remodelled fifteen years later, could hardly be greater.

Opinions differ as to its merits: Pevsner finds in it "none of Pearson's later refinements"; but it earned a laudatory mention in Eastlake's classic history of the Revival (1872), where it is described as "modelled on the earliest and severest type of French Gothic", while the lavish internal carvings, which Pevsner thinks "heavy and demonstrative", represented for Eastlake "scholarly and noble work".

As this drawing shows, the church with its tall, pyramidal spire and adjoining vicarage (also by Pearson) form an impressive silhouette. But it sits a shade uncomfortably in its rural and very English surroundings, the trimness of its lines and the texture of its limestone giving it a bandbox look, as though it had been taken ready made from a mail order catalogue.

Appleton-le-Moors   AD 16.IV.98

St Mary, Kilburn

Lying immediately below the Kilburn White Horse, this sturdy little church is attractively sited at the corner of a small cobbled square opening off the main street. The tower dates only from 1667. The church was heavily restored in the 19th century and much of the fabric is Victorian; but there are traces of its twelfth century origins in the fine Norman chancel arch and south doorway. The bust of a tin-hatted soldier to the right of the gateway into the churchyard is the village war memorial.

The most celebrated Kilburn resident of recent times was Robert Thompson the woodcarver (1876-1955), whose work, usually in oak, always carried a small mouse as his trademark - "a symbol of industry in quiet places". Thompson began his career as the village wheelwright; but a request to make the large wooden cross for the First World War memorial in the Roman Catholic churchyard in Ampleforth village led to his making furniture for the Abbey and College at Ampleforth and so by degrees to becoming one of the most celebrated woodcarvers of his time.

The interior of Kilburn church is full of Thompson's work, and his mouse is to be seen everywhere. The pulpit and faldstool are by him; the pews in the nave are from the workshops in the village where his tradition is carried on; and the side chapel of St Thomas has been furnished in his memory by craftsmen whom he trained. The north aisle also contains some fine old pews dating from the 17th century.

Kilburn

AS 30.1.99

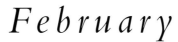

February

St Mary, Bagby

Built in 1862, this is one of five churches in the North Riding by the Victorian architect Edward Buckton Lamb (1806-1869). I have drawn three: Bagby, Aldwark (p.46) and Thirkleby (p.114), all of them out of the ordinary. Lamb also made extensive additions to Nunappleton Hall in the West Riding (since demolished) and built Hughenden in Buckinghamshire for Benjamin Disraeli (Lord Beaconsfield). Pevsner describes him as "the most original though certainly not the most accomplished architect of his day". More kindly, Mark Girouard in *The Victorian Country House* calls him "individual and independent".

As his work here amply demonstrates, Lamb was nothing if not adventurous; and his churches have the rackety charm of conscious eccentricity. At Bagby (as can be seen in this drawing), the crossing is broader than the chancel and incorporates most of the transepts. This accords with Lamb's aim in all his churches, which seems to have been to provide the large central preaching space required for Protestant services within a broadly traditional Gothic structure, adorned with a great deal of what Pevsner calls "mischievous detail". Whatever may be thought of the aesthetic effect, the results are certainly fun to draw.

St. Mary's Church
Bagby
AE 14. viii . 96

All Saints, Brandsby

The handsome cupola of Brandsby church is a pleasant surprise as one comes along the lane which leads from Brandsby to Stearsby. The church dates from 1767, when the then Squire, Francis Cholmeley, decided to pull down the earlier church and replace it on a piece of ground out of sight of the Hall. An amateur architect himself, he employed Thomas Atkinson, of a York family of architects, to produce this severely classical essay.

The exterior is very plain, apart from the cupola. The interior, by contrast, is spacious and elegant, the central space marked out by four tall Tuscan columns supporting the roof on arches, the whole ensemble redolent of 18th century Anglicanism and the Enlightenment, quite unlike any other village church in Ryedale. It was restored in 1905 by Temple Moore, who contributed the pulpit and the fine brass lectern.

Unusually, the Francis Cholmeley who built the church was a Roman Catholic, the Brandsby branch of the Cholmeleys being well-known recusants. There was a chapel in the Hall and a Catholic priest resident in Brandsby from 1604 to 1820. Thereafter, until 1934, the Brandsby Mission was served by the monks of Ampleforth.

The Cholmeleys also had the distinction of being patrons of John Sell Cotman, one of the greatest of English watercolourists, who was introduced to them by another Catholic Squire, Sir Henry Englefield. Cotman visited Brandsby in each of the three years 1802-5 and was treated by the Cholmeleys as a member of the family, so that (in the words of one of his biographers) "the months he spent at Brandsby were the happiest in Cotman's life." Whilst there, he painted numerous scenes at Byland, Rievaulx, Newburgh Priory, Duncombe Park and elsewhere in the North Riding; but it does not appear that he ever painted Brandsby Church.

Brandsby
21·2·99

St Mary, Lastingham

In a countryside rich in beautiful villages, Lastingham is worth a journey, and not just a detour. Sheltered by wooded hills on the south, and lying just below the edge of the open moor to the north, it still has something of that air of being a retreat from the world which brought St Cedd here in 654 to found his monastery where the Norman church now stands.

St Cedd's monastery, visited by Bede in 735, was destroyed by the Danes in the 9th century, but refounded in the 11th by Stephen of Whitby, later first abbot of St Mary's at York. The famous crypt, entered by a flight of modern steps from the nave, is Stephen's work, dating from about 1080. Although it is reputed to have been used in the 18th century for cockfighting, its structure has never been tampered with and even the most hardened materialist is liable to be moved by the sense of primitive devotion which it evokes. The altar is said to be even more ancient than the fabric, and may have been the one on which St Cedd's brother and successor St Chad said Mass.

The crypt is the undoubted glory of Lastingham, but to my mind almost as remarkable is the interior of the main church, with its perfectly rounded apse and magnificent stone vaulting. For this we have mainly to thank J.L.Pearson (see p.8), who restored the church with an exceptional blend of sensitivity and imagination in 1879. Rarely has a Victorian restoration - involving a considerable amount of new construction - succeeded in expressing the spirit of a place so completely as in Pearson's work here at Lastingham.

LASTINGHAM   15. VII. 97

St Nicholas, Husthwaite

The warm, brown masonry of this ancient church is Norman, and inside the porch is a magnificent, deeply incised arch of the early 12th century which forms the south doorway. (The harshly carved, round-arched widows on either side of the porch, however, date from 1896.) To the left of the tower is a glimpse of the Hambleton Hills immediately to the north.

The interior has an equally ancient feel to it, with its rough stone walls - glowing golden in the declining October sun, when I was last there - and low, Norman chancel arch. On the north wall - one in the chancel and one in the nave – are memorial tablets to two 18th century vicars of Husthwaite who were also Masters of the nearby Coxwold Grammar School: Robert Midgeley, who died in 1761 "deservedly admired for his fine taste in classical and polite literature", having "educated several gentlemen who were an honour to their country"; and Robert Pierson, Archdeacon of Cleveland, who died in 1805, whose "classical and botanic knowledge were extensive, and happily adapted to the purity of his taste".

Husthwaite Church

28.7.97

March

St Chad, Sproxton

Ihave always been fond of this essentially 17th century building, which strikes the eye as one comes up the hill towards Helmsley from Malton, backed by two fine copper beeches. It began its existence a mile or so away as the chapel for the long since vanished house of West Newton Grange, having been erected there in the 1640s by Sir Henry Cholmley, a prominent Royalist whose lands were sequestered in 1652. He died at Tangier in 1666, leaving several members of his family buried in a vault beneath the chapel. (The coffins were removed and reinterred at Oswaldkirk in about 1815).

By 1859 the chapel had degenerated into a barn; and in 1879 Vicar Gray of Helmsley (see p.36), as part of his campaign to evangelise the surrounding villages and halt the spread of Dissent, prevailed on Lord Feversham to have it pulled down and re-erected on its present site to serve the cottagers of Sproxton. Most of the furnishings are by Temple Moore, but the interior as well as the exterior retains a pleasantly 17th century flavour.

Across the main road from the church is the Nelson Gate, a triumphal arch which was at one time the principal entrance to Duncombe Park. It is inscribed:

"To the memory of Lord Viscount Nelson, and the unparallelled gallant achievements of the British Navy

Lamented Hero!

O price his conquering country griev'd to pay,

O dear bought glories of Trafalgar's day.

1806"

Sproxton

17.8.97

St John, Howsham

The little village of Howsham, with its magnificent Jacobean Hall, lies just outside Ryedale, across the Derwent from Whitwell-on-the-Hill (p.126). Both have churches by G.E.Street (1824–81), one of the most gifted – and prolific – architects of the Gothic Revival, and it is interesting to compare them.

Of the two, Howsham (built in 1860) is the more ingenious. Eastlake, the historian of the Revival, singled it out for special praise: "there is no better test of an architect's originality...than when he has to deal with the design of a very small village church...Mr Street has shown us how to do this in his design for Howsham Church...He gave the chancel an apsidal end...planned a snug little porch with a lean-to roof for the west end, and carried up a picturesque belfry turret by its side. The effect of the whole is charming." Perhaps 'cheeky' would be a better description.

I found the interior more sympathetic – and successful – than the exterior. Despite its small size it does not seem cramped, the sanctuary being framed in a broad ogival chancel arch and given depth by the apse, while the colour-banded masonry on the walls, the elaborately patterned encaustic floor tiles and the profusion of stained glass, all vivid blues and reds, convey a feeling of restrained sumptuousness. Not to be missed by anyone with a taste for Victorian Gothic.

Howsham

AS 3.3.99

All Saints, Hawnby

The charm of Hawnby church lies in its situation, at the heart of one of the most beautiful and secluded valleys in Ryedale, well away from the village, in the lee of Hawnby Hump. The church is screened by trees and a beck runs alongside the churchyard, which in spring is carpeted with daffodils.

The lane which goes past the church leads to Arden Hall, the site of a pre-Reformation priory of Benedictine nuns suppressed by Henry VIII in 1536. Nothing remains of the priory except a stone chimney breast inside the house, which is now the home of the Earl of Mexborough.

The church itself, restored in the 1870s, retains a Norman doorway but has lost its Norman tower. Inside it is damp, chilly and rather austere. It contains three monuments to members of the Tancred family, who lived at Arden Hall from 1574 to 1900, the earliest being to Ralph Tancred who bought the Hall from the Darcys in 1574 and died in 1601.

Hawnby was also an early centre of Methodism in the North Riding, and in the 1740s local followers of John Wesley tried unsuccessfully to introduce his ideas into the parish church.

According to Wesley (who visited Hawnby himself in 1757), the local landlord - presumably the Tancred of the day - had "turned all the Methodists out of their houses", so that some fifty of them were living in cottages which they had built for themselves "at the end of the town".

Hawnby

17.3.99

St Cuthbert, Crayke

The village of Crayke lies on the side of the only hill to rise from the Vale of York until one comes to the line of the Howardian Hills a couple of miles to the North. The hill is crowned with a castle, once belonging to the Bishops of Durham (though very little of the medieval structure remains); and immediately below the castle, almost on the summit of the hill, stands the church.

Tradition says that St Cuthbert, who died in 687, founded a monastery here; and until 1837 Crayke church was under the jurisdiction of the Bishops of Durham, the village being an exclave of County Durham until 1844. The present church is 15th century, with a wide, low nave and 17th century fittings: a Caroline pulpit dated 1637 with double-nobbed pews (as at Carlton Husthwaite) to match. In the north aisle (added to the church in 1865) is a portrait drawing of Dean Inge of St Paul's ("The Gloomy Dean"), who was born at Crayke in 1860; and a Lady altar of which the medieval altar stone - possibly the original high altar stone - was found in the grounds of the castle.

The ascent to the church is across a large, steeply sloping village green; and from the church porch looking south is a wide view over the plain below. On the summer evening when this drawing was done, the view was at its finest, every detail picked out by the mellow sunshine, with "the splendid pile of York Minster" (to quote Thomas Gill) appearing twelve miles away "like the form of a ship at sea."

Crayke

11.7.99

St Cuthbert, Sessay

An early work of the celebrated William Butterfield (1814-1900), Sessay church stands on rising ground surrounded by open fields, and forms part of a wider composition comprising church, lychgate and school (hidden behind the church in this drawing).

Butterfield was an austere and exacting high churchman ("a thorn in the side of his dazed but obedient employers") who designed no less than 69 churches between 1840 and 1892, his best known memorial being Keble College, Oxford (1868). Here at Sessay, as at Baldersby (p.70) and the nearby village of Dalton, he was working for the 7th Viscount Downe of Baldersby Park,

the son of a parson and the son-in-law of a bishop, who had embraced the Oxford Movement and was an assiduous builder of churches.

What is notable about Sessay church is its harmonious exterior - Butterfield at his simplest and least idiosyncratic - and its peaceful setting; the interior is disappointing and rather bare. In the floor of the chancel is a delicately incised 16th century brass to Thomas Magnus (d.1550), Rector of Sessay and at one time Master of St Leonard's Hospital at York, which he surrendered to King Henry VIII. The 19th century encaustic tiles surrounding it feature the Downe monogram surmounted by a viscount's coronet.

Sessay

$ 8.7.99

April

All Saints, Helmsley

In this view from the top of Church Street, the church silhouette makes an impressively massive backcloth to the row of stone houses on the left. Seen at close quarters, however, its exterior is heavy and somewhat lifeless. Originally Norman, if not Saxon, it was largely rebuilt in the 1860s by Charles Barry junior (son of the architect of the Houses of Parliament).

The interior is more interesting, and on quite a grand scale. It retains important features from the earlier church, including the Norman chancel arch and some finely carved 13th century capitals. The high altar and the panelling of the sanctuary are by Robert Thompson of Kilburn (see p.10) and the ubiquitous Temple Moore was responsible for some of the other furnishings, including the ceiling of the north aisle.

Overall, the church still bears the personal imprint of the Rev Charles Norris Gray, who was vicar of Helmsley from 1870 until his death in 1913, and became a dominating figure in the town. Known universally as "Vicar Gray" (he refused a canonry offered by the Archbishop of York), he was the son of the first Bishop of Cape Town; an outspoken High Churchman, church builder, social reformer, trainer of curates and doughty opponent of dissenters and Roman Catholics. To him we owe the enormous vicarage, now the headquarters of the North York Moors National Park, in which his curates were trained; and also the satellite churches at Pockley (p.54), East Moors (p.70), Carlton (p.96) and Sproxton (p.24). He designed the remarkable series of historical murals in the north aisle and made the chapel in the north transept in memory of his father. He used his energy and position to improve conditions of life for the people of Helmsley both materially and spiritually and the church as it stands today is essentially his memorial.

Helmsley

St Mary, Carlton Husthwaite

A modest little church, attractively sited away from the main street across a small green.

The building is pure 17th century, very plain and simple - inside, just a long, low white-walled hall with double-nobbed Caroline pews (cut down to modern size in 1885) and pulpit dated 1678, simple brass hanging chandeliers to match. The pulpit has an open-work corona characteristic of its date, as is the William and Mary hatchment on the wall; and there is plenty of light from the square-headed windows, giving the whole interior an air of cheerful, unpretentious devotion.

Carlton Husthwaite

$\mathcal{AS}$ 8.7.99

All Saints, Sinnington

Another small church of Norman origin, standing on a hillside overlooking the village, named after the River Seven, which flows peacefully through it. It was extensively restored by the Durham architect Hodgson Fowler in 1904. Although much of the fabric was renewed at that time, it follows the old ground plan and incorporates many of the original features.

The handsome stone porch leads to a Norman doorway, and another arched doorway (blocked up) in the wall beneath the bell-turret is of the same period. Inside, the disproportionately wide chancel arch, which spans virtually the whole width of the nave, dates from the reconstruction of 1904, although here too some of the stonework is old. The communion rail is Jacobean, as are the nobbed benches; but the latter have been altered to make them "comfortable rather than penitential."

Hidden in this drawing, but immediately behind the church to the north, is a large stone barn containing a number of medieval windows. This was originally the great hall of a 12th century manor house, the home of Roger de Clere, a Norman knight from Rouen.

Sinnington

AS 29·IV·98

All Saints and St James, Nunnington

This unpretentious, square-built church stands above the unspoilt village of Nunnington, better known for its 17th century Hall, now the property of the National Trust. The main body of the church dates from the 13th century, but it suffered in the Civil War and was largely rebuilt at the end of the 17th century by Ranald Grahame, who acquired the manors of Nunnington and Stonegrave in 1669. The inevitable Victorian restoration was carried out in 1883/4 by the then Rector, the Rev William Collins, with the lady of the manor, Mrs William Ruston (not Lady Catherine De Bourgh) and her husband meeting most of the cost.

Inside is an effigy of a 14th century knight, believed to be Sir Walter de Teye, who died in 1325. Of interest to the social historian are the memorial tablets to Thomas Jackson, who died in 1766 (in the nave), and Richard Graham, 1st Viscount Preston, who died in 1695 (in the chancel). Jackson was a successful jockey: "well known for his extraordinary performance on the Turf", and the inscription on his tablet informs us that it "affords an useful Lesson to the humble part of mankind who may learn from hence that men of Industry and Honesty may rise to Glory from the lowest station, and have their memories recorded as well as the great and noble."

As a counterpoint to the Newmarket triumphs of the lowly born Mr Jackson, Lord Preston's monument testifies to the honours and vicissitudes of a "great and noble" career. Ambassador to the court of Louis XIV under Charles II, Lord Preston became under James II Secretary of State for Scotland, Master of the Wardrobe and Lord Lieutenant of Cumberland and Westmorland. But in 1688, "upon the landing of the Prince of Orange", he "adhered

20. IV. 98

Nunnington

to the interest of the King his master" and was imprisoned in the Tower. His life being spared, he retired to Nunnington and "dedicated the remainder of his days to...the Service of the King of Heaven."

The epitaph ends on a note resonant with all the romantic devotion the Jacobite cause commanded:

"This noble peer

was blessed with a genius worthy of his High

Descent...

"He was great in the Palace

But greater in the Prison

Where with a Christian Patience and Heroick

Constancy

He stood prepar'd rather to dye for the CROWN,

than desert it".

St Stephen, Aldwark

Like Bagby (p.14) and Thirkleby (p.114), this is by the "rogue" Victorian architect E.B.Lamb. He seems to have been a favourite with Lady Frankland Russell of Thirkleby Park, for whom I think all three churches were built. This one at Aldwark, full of the quirks in which Lamb delighted, is to my mind the most successful of the three.

The church sits in a bend in the road, on gently rising ground overlooking the River Ouse, and giving a wide view over the rolling farmland of the Vale of York. I first came on it early one summer morning, taking a cross-country route to Leeds Airport. The sky was filled with an enormous, shimmering rainbow, which appeared to rise from a field just behind the church, giving it an elfin - almost fairy-like - character.

Its lowness off the ground, the patterning of the stone, brick and flint of which it is built, what Pevsner calls the "weird outline" of the small steeple and indeed the whole composition, are on a human scale, giving it the appearance almost of a toy church. Inside it is friendly and intimate, low again, with a tiny chancel and an elaborately timbered roof. As at Bagby, the transepts are wide and attenuated in length, to give a large central space; but here, each transept ends in an apse-shaped window seat like a big bay-window, which accentuates the domestic feel of the place. All in all, an original building of considerable charm.

St John of Beverley, Salton

East of Helmsley, the flat land which lies between the Moors to the North and the Howardian Hills to the South - the true Rye Dale - is little visited by tourists. In prehistoric times it formed the bed of the vanished lake of Pickering; today it is a pleasant but unremarkable rural landscape of winding lanes, comfortable farms, and small villages through which the Rye meanders on its way to join the Derwent above Malton. Exploring it in a desultory way by car one summer afternoon, I rounded a bend in the lane and came suddenly upon this noble church, glowing warm and honey-coloured in the afternoon sun.

Belonging until the Dissolution to the Augustinian Priory of Hexham in Northumberland, the church in its present form dates from the end of the 12th century, when an earlier church on the same site was destroyed by the Scots. It was rebuilt, only to be ravaged by the Scots a second time in the 14th century, after which it was again repaired.

The windows have been Gothicised and the pyramid cap to the tower was added in the 1840s, but the tower and main fabric are original. The church is entered through a Norman doorway; and the interior has a notable serenity, drawing warmth from the colour of the stone walls and focussing on the altar through the perfect arc of the chancel arch, which is richly decorated with zig-zag carving. A memorial tablet on the north wall to John Dowker (who died in 1816) and his widow Mary, erected by their "numerous offspring" evokes their manifold virtues with touching conviction.

Salton

AS 23.7.98

St Mary the Virgin, Scawton

This tiny church has always been one of my favourites, and I make a practice of stopping to show it to visitors en route to the more spectacular glories of Rievaulx.

Apart from the introduction of additional windows, the structure appears little changed since it was first put up in the 12th century by Roger, the second Abbot of Byland (1141-96), to serve the lay brothers of the abbey living in outlying granges to the north. Attractive but unremarkable on the outside, the church inside has an almost Saxon primitiveness, with its narrow, rounded chancel arch, minute chancel and whitewashed walls.

The feeling of intimacy and warmth which one notices immediately on entering is partly a matter of scale (assisted by the fact, dryly noted in *The Victoria County History*, that "few of the walls are vertical"), but is suggestive also of centuries of prayer and devotion.

The church did in fact undergo a restoration in 1892 at the hands of Hodgson Fowler, to whom Pevsner rightly awards a bouquet for the tact with which he left so much of the original fabric untouched. The result brings us as close to a genuine medieval village church as can be found anywhere in the country.

Until early in the present century the main east-west road to Scarborough passed through Scawton on its way to Helmsley by way of Bow Bridge at Rievaulx; and the village must have been less sleepy and isolated than it now appears. But contemporary history has not entirely passed it by: in the church porch is a memorial to the crew of a Free French bomber, killed in 1945 when their plane crashed near Scawton just before the War ended.

Scawton   4. V. 99

All Saints, Slingsby

Flanked by an imposing Georgian rectory and the ivy-covered ruins of a 17th century castle, this has the mildly imposing appearance of a small collegiate church of the late 15th century. On a second look, the smoothness of its ashlar facing, the regularity of its lines and the consistency of its Perpendicular fenestration betray its Victorian provenance.

Built in 1869 by Admiral Edward Howard at a cost of £5000, it replaced a 15th century church of similar size which had become unsafe. Handsome seems the right word to describe both its dignified exterior and its relatively spacious interior. The discreet lavishness of an affluent patron manifests itself in the quality of the furnishings and the marble shafts of the "Early English" columns which support the chancel arch, while the generosity of the congregation in the 1960s is reflected in the brightly painted ceiling, installed when the entire roof was found to be riddled with dry rot and had to be replaced.

In the Lady Chapel is the effigy of a knight of the Wyville family, variously dated to the mid 13th or early 14th centuries, showing him with his legs crossed and his heart held in his praying hands. A magnificent two-tiered brass corona chandelier, which came from Italy via Sledmere, is a central feature of the nave; and at the back of the church is a memorial tablet listing no less than 101 men from Slingsby - then having a total population of about 500 souls - who served in the First World War, fifteen of whom were killed.

Slingsby

5.V.99

St John Baptist, Pockley

This specimen of high Victorian Gothic by George Gilbert Scott jun. (1839-92) replaced an earlier chapel, said to have been "barnlike" and dating originally from the 13th century. The present church, built in 1870, is another product of Vicar Gray's evangelising energy (see p.36).

The six candlesticks and crucifix on the altar, the alabaster Madonna and Child just inside the chancel and the impressive Rood screen, show that the church continues to reflect Vicar Gray's Anglo-Catholic sympathies. The furnishings are by Temple Moore (who was G.G.Scott's pupil); and the fine crucifixion which tops the rood screen is by Lang of Oberammergau. Altogether a surprisingly elaborate edifice to find in a small moorland village, it would appear to have benefited from the patronage of the Earls of Feversham.

11.5.99

Pockley

June

Holy Trinity, Little Ouseburn

I had no intention of drawing the church of Little Ouseburn or including it in this anthology of North Yorkshire churches. But I happened to be driving past it on my way to Aldwark (p.46) as a June thunderstorm was brewing, and thought that this dramatic glimpse of it across the Ouse Gill Beck against a lowering sky was too good to ignore. The rain came torrenting down as I sat in the car and made my sketch, which may account for the rather notional sheep in the foreground.

This is a genuinely ancient church, the walls and tower largely Norman, with fragments of Saxon masonry built in to them. Inside, the walls have been stripped of plaster, exposing the rough stonework and giving the whole interior a pleasantly primitive feel. The mildly suburban,

half-timbered porch appears to have been erected after the Second World War to commemorate the crew of a Royal Canadian Air Force Halifax bomber which crashed in the adjoining field in March 1945, taking the roof off the church in the process.

Within the churchyard, and clearly visible in this drawing on the right of the church, is the handsome, late eighteenth century mausoleum - a drum-like, domed rotunda with Tuscan pilasters - erected by Henry Thompson of nearby Kirby Hall. Sadly, the hall, in which both Carr of York and the celebrated dilettante Lord Burlington, the disciple of Palladio, had a hand, was pulled down in the 1920s.

8.vi.99

Little Ouseburn

St Columba, Topcliffe

This view was taken on a hot day in August, from a meadow on the opposite side of the River Swale from Topcliffe village. The church stands high above the river, and wears an antique, almost dilapidated look. In reality, only the east window and part of the chancel wall are medieval (of the 14th century); the rest of the church was rebuilt in 1855 by an architect called George Andrews, who specialised in designing railway stations for George Hudson the "Railway King". At closer quarters, it looks substantial, solid and discernibly Victorian.

Inside it is large and lofty, a little bleak and showing signs of wear and tear. In the south wall of the chancel is a window by the youthful Burne-Jones, the Pre-Raphaelite touch already recognisable but not yet fully developed.

Also on the south wall is a large 14th century brass to Sir Thomas de Topcliffe (d.1362) and his wife, of Flemish workmanship.

On the north wall are a clutch of handsome memorials to members of the Robinson family, who later became Earls de Grey and finally Marquesses of Ripon. The largest, an imposing sarcophagus topped by a portrait bust and a quantity of florid decoration, is to Sir Metcalf Robinson bart. (shown in full-bottomed wig, with a lace fichu at his neck), who "livd in great reputation in his country", was three times MP for York, and died in 1688. His descendant, the first Marquess of Ripon (1827-1909), was the only man to be born in No 10 Downing Street - and the only Roman Catholic to be Viceroy of India.

Topcliffe Church

St Peter, Dalby

This unusual church is hard to find, being reached by a bylane opening off the country road which runs along the crest of the Howardian Hills between the villages of Brandsby and Terrington. It is sheltered by trees to the north, but immediately to the south the ground falls steeply away to the plain below, giving a grand view across the Vale of York.

The nave and doorway to the church are Norman; the windows of the nave clearly Victorian and rather crude. But the battlemented and massively buttressed chancel dates from the fifteenth century, when the manor of Dalby was held by the Abbots of St Mary's York. This fortress-like structure, looking like a peel tower with its huge stones and walls four feet thick, is equally massive on the inside, approached through a narrow Norman chancel arch and roofed with a starkly simple barrel vault. It is unique in Ryedale; and I have found nothing to explain why it was thought necessary to protect this particular church in this way. It recalls, on a miniature scale, Sir Walter Scott's description of Durham Cathedral (now inscribed on Prebend's Bridge at Durham):

"...Half Church of God, half castle gainst the Scots".

On the chancel wall are memorial tablets to members of the Plumer family of Lilling Hall which carry eulogy to heights - and lengths - unusual even by early 19th century standards.

St. Nicholas, Dalby

15. viii. 99

Holy Trinity, Stonegrave

Like Kirkdale (p92), Stonegrave church proclaims itself a "Minster" on the ground that a monastic establishment of a somewhat ill defined kind existed here in Saxon times. It had evidently been in existence for some time by AD 757, when it was the subject of a letter from Pope Paul I to King Eadberht of Northumberland. Also dating from well before the Conquest is the impressive Anglo-Celtic cross, now placed inside the church at the rear of the nave, which was found in 1863 built into the chancel wall. Of local stone, it is of a type unique in Ryedale.

The present church is originally of the 12th century, though the external fabric (apart from the tower) is largely Victorian, the building having been heavily restored in 1863. I have drawn it from a number of angles, but I think this view of it from the east best brings out its character, with Oswaldkirk Bank Top just visible behind it.

Inside it is well-proportioned, broad for its overall size, and well worth exploring. Particularly attractive is the light, elegant, open chancel screen, which bears the date 1637. Against the north wall are two medieval tombs with effigies, over which hangs a contemporary portrait of Thomas Comber, Dean of Durham, who died in 1699. His large memorial stone in the floor of the chancel carries a lengthy and laudatory Latin epitaph, which one suspects bears out Dr Johnson's dictum that "in lapidary inscriptions a man is not upon oath."

Connoisseurs of epitaphs will also appreciate the memorial in St Peter's chapel on the south side of the chancel to the wife of an early 19th century curate

Stonegrave Minster

30.7.96

("Renowned as a linguist, critic and divine"), expressed in Latin elegiacs of touching frankness:

"Nec dotata uxor magnisve parentibus orta

"Fida sed, et casta, et semper amata fuit"

That is, she was a wife without dowry or parents of rank, but faithful, chaste and always loved.

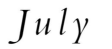

July

All Saints, Hovingham

This ancient church bears witness to the attentions of successive generations of the Worsley family, who have lived in Hovingham since the 16th century. The tower is Saxon, contemporaneous with the Saxon tower at nearby Appleton-le-Street and with St Gregory's Minster at Kirkdale. Hovingham is recorded in Domesday as having belonged before the Conquest to Orm; and this was almost certainly the Orm recorded on Kirkdale's Saxon sundial as having restored the church there "in the days of Edward, the King, and Tostig, the earl" (see p.92).

The main body of the church, however, was rebuilt in 1860, at the expense of one of the Worsleys of the day, by an architect called Rhode Hawkins. He followed the style and ground plan of the earlier church and the building incorporates elements of the original fabric. It contains a number of Worsley memorials, including that of Thomas Worsley (1711-1778), a successor of Sir Christopher Wren as Surveyor-General to the Board of Works, who built the adjacent Hovingham Hall.

A notable feature is the Saxon reredos behind the lady altar: a sculptured stone panel comprising eight arched compartments, each containing a scriptural figure in high relief. Until 1924, when it was moved to its present position, it was embedded in the south wall of the tower. It may originally have been a lintel over a doorway or possibly an altar frontal.

The strikingly modern ordering of the sanctuary was carried out in 1981 as a gift from Sir Marcus and Lady Worsley in memory of Sir William Worsley and his wife. Together with some fine modern stained glass, it testifies to the living character of the church and of the liturgy enacted there.

Hovingham
9. vi. 97

St Mary Magdalene, East Moors

Another of Vicar Gray's satellite churches (see p.36), this charming piece of Victoriana stands among overgrown rhododendrons in rough woodland just off the road to Bransdale and Cokayne, and is almost equally remote. A red telephone box in the bracken by the roadside marks the way in.

Built in 1882, it was Temple Moore's first church and, as Pevsner remarked, "The young architect obviously enjoyed his job thoroughly, and his pleasure is infectious after eighty years." The eighty years are now one hundred and eighteen, but Temple Moore's *jeu d'esprit*, with its stepped bell tower and wagon roof inside, still gives pleasure. John Betjeman celebrated it (in the manner of Burns) in his poem *Perp. Revival i'the North:*

"...a stane kirk wi' a wee spire
> and a verra wee south aisle
The rhododendrons bloom wi'oot
> on ilka Simmer's day
And it's there the Airl o' Feversham
> Wad hae his tenants pray
For there's something in the painted roof
> And the mouldings round the door
The braw bench and the plain font
> That tells o' Temple Moore"

It has grown into its surrounding landscape; and like its companion further up the dale at Cokayne, gives the impression of being much more ancient than it really is.

East Moors

AS 9.8.96

St James the Great, Baldersby

Another Victorian church of exceptional quality, large, gaunt and uncompromising. It stands in open country to the west of Thirsk, and like Sessay (p.32), is by William Butterfield, working for the 7th Viscount Downe of Baldersby Park. Completed in 1858, ten years later than Sessay and on an altogether grander scale, it is unmistakably by the same hand as Keble College, Oxford, which it antedates by another ten years.

Much too large, one would have thought, for a small, country parish, it was erected in the best medieval tradition, to give glory to God rather than with an eye to the pockets or convenience of the parishioners. Butterfield's fondness for "constructional polychromy" - patterning his buildings with contrasting stripes of brick or stone - is much in evidence, both in the banding of the exterior walls and spire and also in the interior, with an abundance of variegated tiling and lavish fittings to match. These include a large and colourful wooden clock, looking for all the world like a cuckoo-clock designed for a giant's nursery.

The 160 foot high pyramidal spire, shown here, is a landmark for miles around in every direction, and a striking example of what has been called Butterfield's "mastery of form".

JS 6. viii. 99

Baldersby
St. James

The Priory Church of St Mary, Old Malton

Even in its present truncated state - comprising the six western bays of the original nave and two thirds of the facade - this is a noble church, dating from the twelfth century. Inside, the fine Norman arches and lofty roof give a sense of space and splendour; the facade, apart from the fifteenth century central window, is early English, with a magnificent Norman doorway.

Old Malton was a Gilbertine priory, belonging to the only medieval religious order of English origin. The Gilbertines were founded in the twelfth century by Gilbert of Sempringham, a parish priest in Lincolnshire, originally as an order of nuns; but to these Gilbert added lay brothers and lay sisters on the Cistercian model, and then male canons on the Augustinian model, to serve as chaplains to the nuns.

Most Gilbertine priories were "double" houses - ie comprising both nuns and canons - with a nun as superior. (The male and female communities were housed separately and had only the church in common). Old Malton, however, was for men only, and at its largest had 30 canons and 35 laybrothers.

After the Dissolution, the church became a parish church, but one too large for the parish to maintain. The central tower fell in 1636, and more of the fabric collapsed in the course of the 18th century. It was restored and re-modelled by Temple Moore in 1889.

The Gilbertines ran hospitals, orphanages and alms-houses and like the Cistercians, derived much of their income from sheep farming. The order grew rapidly (although it never spread beyond England), and by the end of the twelfth century there were more than a dozen Gilbertine priories in the country, all but two of which were double houses of nuns and canons. At the time of the Dissolution, there were twenty-five houses, the majority of them in the north and east of the country.

St. Mary's Priory
Old Malton

7.7.99

The last Master of Sempringham (as the Head of the order was called) was Robert Holgate, who became an enthusiastic supporter of the Reformation. Made Archbishop of York under King Edward VI in 1545, he did all he could to foster Protestantism in York, founded Archbishop Holgate's School (which still flourishes) and was deprived of his see by Queen Mary in 1554 for having married.

August

St Oswald, Oswaldkirk

The dedication of the church to St Oswald (c.605-642), King of Northumbria, together with the fact that the village is named after the church and mentioned as such in Domesday, is testimony to its Saxon origins.

I first drew it in 1950, when I was a schoolboy, from the same vantage point as here; and as far as I can see the intervening 47 years effected no change of any kind. It looks now as it did then, backed by the thick woodland of Oswaldkirk Hag, a compact little village church with traces of its early origins and later history plainly discernible under a tidy 19th century veneer.

The adjoining late Georgian rectory, however, where I remember the then Rector telling me how his stipend had fallen in consequence of the nationalisation of the railways, is now an elegant private house and a rectory no longer.

Inside the church, at the back of the nave, is a curious triple arch supporting the belltower, apparently dating from the church's restoration in 1886. The Jacobean pulpit is supposed to be that from which Archbishop Tillotson, a formidable 17th century preacher against both popery and dissent, gave his first sermon; and there is the tomb slab of an (unknown) abbot of Byland in the floor to the north of the altar. The south doorway has two finely carved Norman capitals; and in the porch (recently erected, according to Thomas Gill in 1852, "at very considerable expense") is an early carving of the virgin and child of about 1000.

When I was last there, the ladies of the parish were busy festooning it with flowers and vegetables for the Harvest Festival - another reassuringly unchanging element in English village life.

13. VIII. 97

Oswaldkirk

St Helen and the Holy Cross, Sheriff Hutton

St Helen, mother of the Emperor Constantine, is credited with having discovered the true cross on which Our Lord was crucified: hence the dedication of this rugged country church, which stands at the furthest end of the village from the gaunt ruins of the castle. The irregular roofline and the different colours and contrasting textures of the stonework - grey limestone mixed in with honey-coloured sandstone - testify to successive additions and alterations to what was originally a Norman foundation.

The subsequent history of the church is bound up with that of the castle, built by John Lord Neville of Raby at the end of the 14th century to replace an earlier one dating from about 1140. The castle came into the possession of King Richard III, which explains the church's most notable monument: a richly carved alabaster effigy and tomb-chest in the St Nicholas (north) side-chapel of a small boy, robed and coroneted. This is believed to be the tomb of Edward, Prince of Wales, Richard III's son by Anne Neville, who died at Middleham in 1484 aged 11. Also in this chapel is the effigy of Sir Edward Thweng, killed in the Scottish Wars in 1334, and a brass commemorating the founder of the chapel, Thomas Bytham (died 1474), who was Chancellor of the Exchequer to Henry VI and Edward IV.

The interior of the church is as varied and rambling as the exterior, adorned with some handsome memorial tablets and still filled with (mainly 19th century) box-pews, several of them roomy enough to accommodate an entire family.

Sheriff
Hutton

3·X·98

All Saints, Old Byland

On the mellow, tranquil evening in late summer when this drawing was done, Old Byland seemed the epitome of all the small, remote moorland churches of Ryedale, redolent of isolation, antiquity and devotion. In the *Victoria County History* its dedication is said to have been unknown, so the attribution to All Saints must be recent. Its absolute simplicity is relieved by the unusual porch-tower, crowned by a nicely curlicued weather-cock.

A wooden church is recorded in Domesday as having existed here in 1085, when Helmsley and Old Byland were the only settlements in this part of Ryedale to have survived William the Conqueror's "harrowing of the North". This was evidently replaced by a very early Norman structure, fragments of which (including two carved dragons) can be seen around the doorway into the porch. Also built into the porch wall on the south side is a small Saxon sundial, allegedly inscribed "Sumar-ledan me facit".

In its present form, the church is mainly twelfth century, probably built by the monks of Byland Abbey during their short sojourn near here, before they moved to Oldstead and thence to their final home near Wass. It remained in the possession of Byland until the Dissolution of the Monasteries. In more recent times it has benefited from the support of the Wombwells of Newburgh, to whom the entire village of Old Byland belonged until 1922. The chancel was restored by Sir George Wombwell in 1909, and re-roofed in 1982 by Captain Malcolm Wombwell (who is commemorated in a tablet on the north wall of the nave), when the 15th century roof-beams were exposed.

Old Byland

10.8.96

All Hallows, Sutton-on-the-Forest

A dignified parish church in the centre of an unusually elegant village, almost facing the wrought iron gates of the chastely Georgian Sutton Park. Lawrence Sterne was vicar here from 1738 until his death in 1768, but from 1760 he lived at Coxwold (see p.108), which he preferred. The 'Forest' incorporated in the name of this village, and also of Marton (p.104), is the old Royal Forest of Galtres, which had effectively disappeared by the end of the Civil War.

The church was extensively reconstructed in the 1870s, but without detriment to its appearance. The chancel is spacious and airy, well lit by the square-headed Perpendicular (15th century) windows shown in this drawing. The pulpit is one from which Sterne probably preached; and there are several fine 18th century memorial tablets to members of the Harland family of Sutton Park, one being to Richard Harland who fought for the King at Marston Moor, and under the Commonwealth "suffered fines and imprisonment until the year 1660, when Monarchy, Religion and Liberty were restored together".

Sutton on the Forest

The Abbey Church of St Laurence, Ampleforth

The monastic community now at Ampleforth traces a tenuous descent from the community of Westminster Abbey under Queen Mary, which was dissolved by Queen Elizabeth I in 1559; and in the wall to the south of the sanctuary is a tile from Westminster and an inscription: "Attendite ad petram unde excisi estis": 'Remember the rock from which you have been hewn'. The community came properly into existence, however, only in 1608, when a group of English Benedictine monks, unable to settle in England because of the penal laws against Roman Catholics, established a priory at Dieulouard, near Nancy, in Lorraine. There they remained until the French Revolution, sending monks across the Channel to act as missionary priests in England.

In 1793, the French authorities confiscated the priory and expelled the monks, who had no choice but to return to England. One of their number, Fr Anselm Bolton, who had been chaplain and steward to Lady Anne Fairfax at Gilling Castle, was living in retirement in a house she had built for him at Ampleforth; and it was here, after wandering the country for nine years in search of a home, that the tiny handful of monks still remaining finally settled in 1802 and opened a small school. Today the community has around one hundred monks (many of them serving parishes away from the monastery) and the school over five hundred boys.

The present Abbey church, designed by Sir Giles Gilbert Scott, was started in 1922 but completed only in 1961, after his death. Its massive central tower dominates the valley and helps to unify the amorphous assemblage of school and monastic buildings on either side of it – although its visual impact has been diminished by the fussy

Ampleforth Abbey Church

facade and roofline of the new (1989) central building immediately to the east of it (fortunately not visible in this drawing).

The monks' stalls are of oak, by Robert Thompson of Kilburn; and the great crucifix over the High Altar was the subject of the agnostic Arnold Toynbee's dream, described in *A Study of History*, in which he found himself clinging to the foot of the cross and hearing a voice saying *Amplexus expecta:* hold on and wait.

Pevsner thought the church lacking in the "zest and originality" of Scott's cathedral at Liverpool. Most people, however, find its massive simplicity impressive. Inside, although Gothic in detail, it is Romanesque in feeling, having been inspired by the Romanesque cathedral of S. Front at Périgueux in the Dordogne. There is a marked contrast between the elaborately carved detail of the monks' choir and altar canopy, which date from the 1920s, and the 1950s austerity of the rest; and the relationship of the different shapes and levels of vaulting is uncomfortable. But, as with many less than satisfactory buildings, its charms grow with familiarity. It has acquired the patina of prayer; and when shafts of sunlight are falling on the sanctuary and the west window is full of glowing colour, the interior seems all space and light.

September

St Giles, Skelton

Although now almost a suburb of York, Skelton keeps its village character, its green fringed by ancient trees, and its small jewel of a church, correctly described in the local guide-leaflet as "one of the most perfect thirteenth century parish churches in England".

What makes it so is its completeness: pure Early English in style throughout, with narrow lancet windows, much dog-tooth moulding and a lavishly carved doorway, it was evidently built in its entirety around 1240 by masons employed on York Minster and has undergone no fundamental alteration since. The doorway was sensitively restored early in the 19th century by a gifted mason called Michael Taylor and the roof was replaced in a further restoration of the church in 1846. The interior walls are no longer painted, as they would have been in the middle ages, the rood screen has gone, and although the two side chapels remain, they no longer contain altars. For the rest, the church looks almost exactly as it must have looked when it was finished: a miniature building of the highest quality, in many respects more like the side chapel of a cathedral than a parish church.

On the day I drew it, a wedding was taking place there and my view was momentarily blocked by a carriage and pair bringing the bride and adding to the illusion of timelessness.

Skelton

AS 17. 7. 99

St Gregory's Minster, Kirkdale

Tucked away in the narrow, wooded valley of the Hodge Beck, this well-loved little church impresses by the beauty of its setting and by the air of antiquity which pervades it. That successive alterations and additions have turned it into an architectural muddle in no way detracts from its charm or its interest.

Saxon in origin, it was added to or partly rebuilt in the 12th, 13th and 15th centuries; the tower was added in the early 19th century; the chancel was put on in 1881; and a major restoration was carried out under the direction of Temple Moore in 1907.

Its most famous feature is the ancient stone sundial set above the south doorway, under cover of the porch. It bears a clearly legible Anglo-Saxon inscription, which records that "Orm, Gamal's son, bought St Gregorius Minster when it was all broken and fallen down, and he had it built anew from the ground to Christ and St Gregory in the days of Edward, the King, and Tostig, the earl." This establishes that the church was rebuilt in the decade 1055-1065, when King Harold's brother Tostig was earl of Northumberland; and shows that there was an earlier church on the same site. The south and west walls of the nave survive from Orm's church, together with parts of the columns supporting the chancel arch.

Notable among the memorials on the inside walls of the church is a fine modern cartouche with scalloped edges, armorial bearings, dignified Roman lettering and a lapidary conclusion ("Artis Desiderium Vitae Felicitas"). It commemorates Sir Gervase Beckett, baronet, of Kirkdale Manor, who died in 1937.

KIRKDALE

27.8.96

St Michael, Cold Kirby

The small upland village of Cold Kirby comprises a single long, broad street of cottages terminating with this sturdy, unpretentious church. Beyond the church (from where this drawing was done), the ground falls away to reveal fold upon fold of moor to the north and east.

Before the Reformation, the church belonged first to the Knights Templars and then to the Knights Hospitallers; and the tower has the rugged solidity which one might associate with a military order. In fact however the church was completely rebuilt in 1841 by Mr Thomas Duncombe of Copgrove and Cold Kirby, a local squire.

The interior has something of the flavour of an early Victorian workhouse: starkly simple, with whitewashed walls, a heavy, rounded chancel arch and no ornament except for a laudatory memorial tablet to Mr Thomas Duncombe. When I last visited it - on a bleak morning in January - both the church and its setting gave the impression of having escaped from the pages of *Wuthering Heights*.

Cold Kirby

St Aidan, Carlton

Another of Vicar Gray's satellite churches and, like East Moors (p.70), by the young Temple Moore. Carlton is the last village as one goes north from Helmsley into the high moors, and the church stands at its northern end, like a sentinel. From the outside, it looks French, with its plain tower topped by a red-tiled, pyramidal cap. Inside, its thick whitewashed walls, narrow slit windows, simple wooden screen and barrel roof make it a model of rural simplicity, at once austere and satisfying. The twin churches of East Moors and Carlton demonstrate that the architect could be as skilful and sensitive on a small scale, using only basic materials, as in the larger, more ornate projects in which practitioners of the Gothic Revival delighted.

October

St Mary, Leake

No motorist using the main A19 road between Thirsk and Teesside can miss this ancient church standing in open ground only a hundred yards or so from the southbound carriageway. The only dwelling anywhere near it is the seventeenth century manor house of Leake Hall (now a farm); for the village of Leake had already disappeared in 1086, and is believed to have been destroyed at the time of the Conquest. The church now serves the neighbouring villages of Silton, Knayton and Borrowby.

The volume of traffic hurtling up and down the A19, and the speed at which it travels, mean that courage is needed to make the sharp turn into the narrow lane which gives access both to the church and the farm. But it is worth the risk. The church is as ancient as it looks, with its arcaded early Norman tower (from which the parapet has disappeared) giving it an almost Saxon appearance. To judge from an amateur watercolour drawing of it done in 1817, the exterior has changed little, if at all, since the 18th century. Indeed it looks today much as it must have done at the time of the Reformation. (Not so the A19, which appears in the watercolour as a rough track, empty except for a couple of travellers on a single horse.)

The interior is much lighter than one would expect for a small country church of such antiquity, most of it no later than the early fourteenth century. It is lovingly maintained, the proportions of nave and chancel seem just right and there is a feeling of warmth which comes from the honey-coloured sandstone of which the church is built. The communion rail is made from the old rood screen and the choir stalls have beautifully carved bench-ends which tradition says came from Rievaulx Abbey.

Leake
Church
24·xi·94

St Mary, Raskelf

Raskelf church lies at the end of the village, giving on to fields which were once the park of a great house (long vanished) belonging to the Nevills, Earls of Westmorland. Its most distinctive feature is its wooden bell-tower, which smacks of East Anglia rather than North Yorkshire, and which is thought to date from the 15th century. The friendly interior too is notable for its woodwork, the fine, broad chancel arch being of wood and the chancel roof and side-screen both incorporating medieval timbers.

A drawing dated 1820 which hangs at the back of the nave shows the church in a state of dilapidation, the wooden tower lacking its pointed cap and the nave apparently roofless; so much of the present fabric is Victorian (1879), and the tower was last restored as recently as 1954. But the north arcade is Norman; the communion rails and font cover are 17th century; and, as noted above, some of the other woodwork is medieval. In the north chapel (now used as a vestry) is one of the many reminders of imperial service overseas which are to be found in English village churches: a memorial tablet to Augustus Webb, a captain in the 17th Lancers and brother to the then squire of Raskelf, who died at Scutari of wounds received in the Charge of the Light Brigade.

Raskelf

24. 7. 97

St Mary, Marton-in-the-Forest

A strange little church on the edge of a hamlet too small to appear on most motoring maps, it was connected with the now vanished Augustinian priory of Marton two miles or so to the northwest, of which the the foundations can be traced in a field immediately to the east of the road from Brandsby to Stillington.

Gill, no doubt going partly by its weatherbeaten appearance and the Saxon-looking simplicity of its interior, says that the church "bears the marks of great antiquity". It would seem that the small chancel is of Norman origin; but according to the *Victoria County History* the rest of the church, including the tower and very odd stepped gables, was rebuilt in about 1546, probably incorporating carvings and other materials from the dissolved priory. Over the doorway is a crudely carved and partly obliterated angel with outstretched wings.

Despite the adjoining farm buildings, the church has an air of pleasantly romantic desolation, crouching down in its unmown graveyard against the long, gentle line of the Howardian Hills to the North.

Marton in the Forest

1.9.96

St Mary, Alne

Although the top of the tower is unmistakably Georgian ("marking the tasteless style of 1766", in the Victorian judgement of Thomas Gill), and the windows of the nave are 15th century, this large, square-looking church is basically Norman. It is recovering from several years of neglect, when it was without a vicar; but energetic parishioners have refurbished it, installed a new clockface and tidied the large churchyard.

Its most remarkable feature is the Norman doorway, visible in this drawing, the inner and outer arches of which are filled with exuberant carvings. Those on the outer arch constitute a bestiary, the names of the beasts being given in Latin ("Vulpis", "Panthera", "Aquila" etc). On the inner arch are some of the Signs of the Zodiac intermingled with sacred imagery including the lamb, and the pelican giving blood from its breast. A mermaid being pursued by a sea monster is discernible on one of the capitals.

Just across the road is the entrance to Alne Hall, formerly the home of the Strangwayes family, which in 1956 became the first Cheshire Home in the north of England and continues to flourish in that capacity.

St. Mary, Alne

St Michael, Coxwold

Like the broad, beautifully harmonious village street which it dominates, Coxwold Church is redolent of squirearchy. Outwardly all of a piece - Perpendicular, of the 15th Century - and crowned by its unusual octagonal tower, its interior reflects the history of the Belasyse and Wombwell families who have lived at nearby Newburgh Priory from its dissolution as a monastery in 1539 down to the present.

The wide, aisleless nave with its box pews (including the squire's family pew at the front), the tablets to the Wombwell sons who died in India and South Africa, the Royal Coat of Arms over the chancel arch flanked on either side by the armorial bearings of the Belasyse Earls, and above all the chancel itself, crowded with the disproportionately grandiose Belasyse tombs, perfectly encapsulate the vanishing world of rural feudalism. As Laurence Sterne (who held the living of Coxwold for

seven years from 1760) dryly observed; "You can see that it is the house of my Lord".

The Wombwells (who acquired Newburgh by marriage with a Belasyse heiress in 1791) have presided over Coxwold through several generations and their monogram and crest can be seen on the gables of farmhouses and cottages throughout the neighbourhood. When my wife and I first came to Ampleforth, old people in the village still remembered Sir George Wombwell, the fourth baronet, who died in 1913. As a young ensign in the 17th Lancers, he had ridden in the charge of the Light Brigade and then ruled over Coxwold for fifty years, improving his estate, hunting with the York and Ainsty and acting as host to King Edward VII.

Fortuitously, this drawing also records a royal event, but a sad one: done in September 1979, it shows the flag of St George flying at half-mast for Earl Mountbatten,

D.G. 4. IX. 79.

COXWOLD

murdered by the IRA eight days earlier. A humbler note is struck in the church porch, where a copper plate on the wall records in Latin the death in 1651 of Elizabeth Faucon, aged 23, who died on that spot while awaiting the arrival of her betrothed.

Laurence Sterne is buried immediately to the right of the church porch; and it was here, in the old brick vicarage on the edge of the village which he christened Shandy Hall, that he wrote "Tristram Shandy" and the "Sentimental Journey".

November

All Saints, Appleton-le-Street

Like the mast of a ship, the unmistakably Saxon tower of Appleton church rides high above the village as you approach it along the road from Malton. It appears to have been built in two or three stages, the earliest dating from before the Conquest and the top tier from just after it. The body of the church is Saxon too, with the chancel and north aisle added in the 13th century and the south aisle (seen in this drawing) around 1300.

In 1346 a chantry chapel was established in the south aisle by Sir Thomas de Boulton, and there are stone effigies of two fourteenth century Boulton ladies in the sanctuary, one on each side of the high altar. The altar rails and altar table were installed in 1636. In the tower wall above the entrance porch is a finely carved but decapitated medieval statue of the Virgin and child, desecrated at the Reformation.

Everything about Appleton church has an ancient feel to it, and it is thought that it may stand on the site of a pagan temple.

Appleton-le-Street   JS 22.viii.97

All Saints, Thirkleby

The twin villages of Great and Little Thirkleby lie just off the busy A19 road from York to Teesside, hidden from it by a ridge of higher ground on which stands the parish church. Its story is bound up with that of the Frankland family (made baronets by Charles II) who were squires of Thirkleby until well into the 20th century. With their departure, Thirkleby Hall (by James Wyatt) was pulled down so that today only the entrance arch and stables survive.

The church too has undergone more than one sea-change, the present Victorian building being the third on the site. The first church, said to have dated from the 12th century, was pulled down in 1722 by the Sir Thomas Frankland of the day, and replaced by one "in the Italian style". This in turn was pulled down in 1850 by Lady Frankland Russell, who replaced it with the present one in memory of her husband.

As at Aldwark (p.46), which also belonged to the Franklands, and Bagby (p.14), the architect was the vigorous eccentric E.B. Lamb, who produced here one of his spikiest churches, with its tall narrow spire and sharply angled roof: in Pevsner's words, "a veritable riot of forms, perverse and mischievous". Time, however, mellows all things, and today, isolated both from the village and the main road, and approached through a tunnel of overgrown yews, the church has an air of venerable seclusion. But its silhouette, equally striking whether seen against the western sky or (as in this drawing) against the low line of moors to the east, could only be Victorian.

The interior incorporates a profusion of Frankland memorial tablets from the two earlier churches, bearing witness, as in so many village churches, to the involvement of local families in the business of empire: Henry Frankland, "Governor of Fort William, in Bengal"; Sir

Thirkleby

26.7.96

Charles Frankland who was (according to Gill) "for many years collector of His Majesty's Customs for the port of Boston, North America" and afterwards Consul-General in Portugal, where "he was buried for an hour under the ruins in the great earthquake at Lisbon": and, in a little apsidal side chapel (a sort of Protestant chantry), a tablet to a naval Frankland who captured a valuable French ship off Havana, became an Admiral of the White and was MP for Thirsk in five successive parliaments.

St Hilda's, Ampleforth

Long and low, with its small, squat tower, St Hilda's, like the village it serves, is sheltered to the north by the escarpment of the moors, and looks south across the valley to the western spur of the Howardian Hills. Norman, with a 13th century chancel, the church was heavily restored in 1868 and the interior looks predominantly Victorian - or did so until recently, when a drastic reordering was carried out to meet modern liturgical requirements. The chancel has been stripped of its Victorian furnishings and screen, and a new, free-standing altar installed almost on the chancel steps.

An odd feature of the church is a mid-14th century monument of a recumbent knight, from behind whose shoulder a wimpled lady appears, smiling a faint but knowing smile. At one time thought to be the effigy of a knight killed at the Battle of Byland (1332) and being comforted by his wife, it is now without any satisfactory explanation.

Although the Fairfaxes of Gilling were lords of the manor, Ampleforth never had a squire. Most of the villagers were small freeholders (or poachers and ne'er-do-wells expelled from the neighbouring estate villages of Coxwold, Gilling and Oswaldkirk), so the only memorials in the church are to yeoman families and one of their relations: Captain William Easterby of the Dragoon Guards, who served under Wellington in the Low Countries, but just missed the Battle of Waterloo.

A modern headstone near the church door marks the grave of two villagers who deserve to be remembered: Noel Appleby and his wife Diana. Noel Appleby served in the Royal Engineers in the first World War, when he captained a paddle steamer on the River Tigris; and subsequently ran the village garage at Ampleforth for fifty years. A self-taught polymath fascinated by local history, he brought electricity to the village, operated a bus and taxi service, ran a fleet of traction engines delivering coal to the surrounding villages, and was an expert repairer of antique clocks. His wife Diana, a collateral descent of Captain Easterby, looked after any injured bird or animal that was brought to her, which then usually became an inmate of the house. On one occasion the Applebys asked the village doctor to treat an injured magpie. When Appleby offered to pay him, Dr Vidal famously replied: "Put your money back in your pocket, Appleby; I'd sooner treat your bird than most of my human patients."

AS 4.IX.98

St. Hilda's Church
Ampleforth

St Nicholas and St Mary, Bransdale

Perhaps the most beautifully situated of all the churches on this pilgrimage, this little building lies, half hidden by woods, on a hillside at the head of Bransdale, 9½ miles into the moors from Helmsley at a spot called Cokayne. From the porch, there is a magnificent view down almost the full length of the dale towards Kirkbymoorside.

The building has a primitive air which belies the fact that it is said to date only from 1886, when it replaced a much earlier structure known as "the old Cockan chapel" and referred to as "Cocken Kirke" in 1538. But the sparsely furnished interior evokes the Anglicanism of the 17th rather than the 18th or 19th centuries; and one can imagine George Herbert here, praying for his country parishioners and reflecting in solitude on Christ's Passion:

"Love is that liquor sweet and most divine
"Which my God feels as bloud: but I as wine".

Among the 18th century gravestones in the churchyard is that of Thomas Gowlan, who died in 1768 aged 29. His epitaph, inscribed on a copper plate screwed to the headstone, reads:

"Afflictions sore
long time I bore
Physicians were in vain
When GOD did please
then Death did ease
and quit me of my pain".

That this was, in its day, a standard verse appearing on gravestones all over the country does not detract from its pathos in the case of a young man aged only 29 at the time of his death.

St. Nicholas, Bransdale

AS 25.VIII.99

December

St Nicholas, Stillington

A friendly-looking church with a small tower, standing on a bank above the long village street, St Nicholas, Stillington, catches the eye of anyone driving along the main country road from Helmsley to York. From the outside, it looks like a comfortable 15th century village church; in reality it was largely rebuilt in the 1840s, in the style (and no doubt using the materials) of the earlier church.

Inside, its early Victorian character becomes more apparent in the uncompromisingly plastered and whitewashed walls, the starkly arcaded nave and the black roof-beams. It is beautifully kept, the brass gleaming, the whole church carpeted, and full of light from the Perpendicular windows. The box pews, with their latched doors, are an attractive feature. But neither in atmosphere nor charm does the interior quite live up to the promise of the exterior.

STILLINGTON

18.IX.98

St John Evangelist, Whitwell-on-the-Hill

Like the church at Howsham (p.26), and built at the same time (1860), this is the work of G.E.Street, the architect of the Law Courts on the Strand in London.

As can be seen from the picture, it makes a dramatic silhouette, which is what led me to draw it in a grey wash rather than in colour. The tower, with its broach spire, is a landmark for miles around and is clearly visible from the Wolds. The body of the church, comprising a nave and chancel, is smaller than might be expected from the size and height of the steeple; and the interior is handsome of its kind but relatively conventional. There are memorial tablets to the fourth Earl of Liverpool, a Lord in Waiting to Queen Victoria, and his son (who was killed in Mesopotamia in 1916); and also to Sir Edmund Lechmere (who died in 1894) and his wife, the co-founders of the church.

The drawing was done on a warm day in August, but I have allocated a place here because the patronal feast of St John the Evangelist is on 27 December.

WHITWELL-ON-THE-HILL

AS 15.viii.1997

Christ the Consoler, Skelton-on-Ure (Newby Church)

In 1870 Frederick Vyner, aged 23, brother to the then owner of Newby Hall, was murdered by brigands in Greece. His mother, Lady Mary Vyner, decided to put the compensation money offered by the Greek Government towards the erection of this church in her son's memory; and his brother-in-law Lord Ripon built a similar memorial church at Studley Royal.

The architect chosen for both churches was William Burges (1827-1881), who had designed St Finbar's Cathedral at Cork and recreated Cardiff Castle for the Marquess of Bute. Burges believed in a close union between architecture, painting and sculpture and was a master craftsman in the design of furniture, plate and jewellery. (Evelyn Waugh was an ardent admirer, and collector, of furniture by Burges). When, as here, he had a patron with unlimited funds, the result was a building of sumptuous opulence, every surface covered with sculpture or rich materials such as alabaster (used here to panel the chancel).

The sculpture inside and outside the church, including the elaborate Ascension over the chancel arch is by T. Nicholls, who also worked with Burges at Cork. Worth noting amid the profusion of statuary are the delicate angels in the soffit (underside) of the chancel arch, ascending and descending by Jacob's ladder.

Vanbrugh's famous epitaph

"Lie heavy on him earth, for he

"Laid many a heavy load on thee"

could apply equally to Burges. At Newby, the church seems to crouch down on the earth, loaded with masonry and carving, the interior full of dark, jewelled colour, the chancel low and cavernous in relation to the nave, like a

Newby
Church

2.IX.97

subterranean treasure-house. Together with its companion church at Studley, it must rank as one of the most splendid and complete examples of Victorian church architecture in Britain. The effect is magnificent but, for those with austerer tastes, overwhelming.

Its dedication to "Christ the Consoler" (as far as I know unique) seems to make it a suitable choice for Christmas Day.

The Abbey of the Blessed Virgin Mary at Byland

Having begun the year with Rievaulx, it seems appropriate to end it with the other great Ryedale abbey ruin of Byland. Like Rievaulx, this was drawn on a crisp. bright winter's morning (two days after Christmas), after a night of snow.

The monastic community at Byland was an offshoot of the Savignac abbey at Furness, in Cumbria. Their first home in Yorkshire was at Hood Grange, in the shadow of Hood Hill and the Devil's Leap, whence they moved to Old Byland. There they soon found that they were too close to Rievaulx, and that the bells of the two monasteries disturbed one another; so in 1147 they migrated to Oldstead and finally, in 1177, through the generosity of Roger de Mowbray, to their "Bella Landa", the modern Byland. Meanwhile the order of Savigny had been assimilated into that of Citeaux, so it was as Cistercians that they moved into their new home.

Although the buildings at Byland follow broadly the same standard Cistercian plan as at Rievaulx, the feel of the place is quite different. Compared to Rievaulx, penned in its narrow, wooded valley, Byland hardly seems to be in a valley at all. The well-wooded slopes of the Hambleton Hills form a backcloth, but the abbey itself lies in open country and the sense of tranquillity which pervades it comes more from space than from seclusion.

Less dramatically situated and much less visited than Rievaulx, Byland, despite its closeness to the road, is often virtually deserted and can be explored and enjoyed in solitude. The pointing finger of its single, surviving pinnacle, beside the lower curve of what was once a great rose window, gives it a uniquely distinctive silhouette, and the western facade is unchanged since Cotman painted it early in the 19th century.

The site was drained and cleared and the building work begun while the monks were still at Oldstead, and most of what remains dates from the late 12th and early 13th centuries. Although the community was never as large as at Rievaulx, the church is said to be the largest Cistercian church in England and the cloister the largest in the North.

27. XII. 96

Byland
Abbey